100

CW00404791

JUMPERS TO FOLLOW 2019-20

Fifty eighth year of publication

Edited by James Norris

First published in 2019 by Raceform Ltd
27 Kingfisher Court, Hambridge Road, Newbury, Berkshire, RG14 5SJ

Copyright © Raceform Ltd 2019

A CIP catalogue record for this book is available from the British Library

ISBN 978-1-83950-015-2

Printed and bound in Great Britain by RHL Print, Swindon

100 WINNERS
JUMPERS TO FOLLOW 2019-20
(ages as at 2019)

A PLUS TARD (FR) 5 b g

Before joining Henry de Bromhead, A Plus Tard raced exclusively in France, picking up a Listed handicap hurdle on his final outing in that country. He was beaten a neck on Irish debut, which was also his first run over fences. The next start saw him get off the mark as a chaser, with subsequent Arkle winner Duc Des Genievres back in second, but he was then beaten in a Grade 3. It was his next performance that saw him take a huge step up the ladder, landing the Close Brothers Novices' Handicap Chase at the Cheltenham Festival by 16 lengths. He wasn't quite at his best on his final run before a summer off, which was his first start in a Grade 1, but he'll no doubt come back refreshed this season with potential at the top level. HENRY DE BROMHEAD

ABACADABRAS (FR) 5 b g

A classy bumper performer last term, Abacadabras ought
to be capable of having a big say in the novice hurdling
division for his top team. He ran out when likely to be
second behind Envoi Allen in February at Leopardstown but
looked straightforward in two runs afterwards, including an
eyecatching fourth in the Champion Bumper. He's bred to
enjoy stepping up beyond the minimum and, while winter
ground shouldn't pose too much of an issue, the five-year-old
does seem particularly happy on a sound surface.
GORDON ELLIOTT

AL BOUM PHOTO (FR) 7 b g

A promising novice chaser the season before last, Willie
Mullins' gelding fulfilled that promise and rewarded ante-
post followers of this publication with a fine win in the 2019
Cheltenham Gold Cup. His season did not begin until January,
when he gave weight and a beating to six useful rivals, headed
by previous Ladbrokes Trophy (formerly Hennessy) winner
Total Recall. His next start was at Cheltenham, where he
ran out a convincing winner from a strong field. His only
subsequent run was in the Punchestown Gold Cup, in which
he made several mistakes before chasing home stablemate
Kemboy, the pair miles clear of the rest. He is likely to face a
strong challenge from that rival in defending his title, but he
is still only a seven-year-old with just 13 races behind him.
There is every chance he has not yet reached his peak.
WILLIE MULLINS

ALLAHO (FR) 5 b g

Allaho's opening second-placed finish in 2018 at Auteuil was
promising, but his debut for Willie Mullins in a bumper 297
days later was slightly underwhelming, coming home fourth

at Leopardstown over 2m. However, following a 50-day break, his attention was turned to hurdling, and he won in great style stepped right up to 3m. Connections were then tempted to send him to the Albert Bartlett despite his inexperience, where he claimed an honourable third. He followed that with a second in a 3m Grade 1 event at Punchestown before his summer off. It's hard to be certain whether hurdling or chasing is on the agenda this time round, but he's open to improvement and will be hard to beat wherever he turns up. WILLIE MULLINS

ANDY DUFRESNE (IRE) 5 b g

Andy Dufresne featured in this book last year when yet to race under rules. He had changed hands for a lot of money having won his sole start in points but the son of Doyen wasn't seen until January 2019, when in the famous green and gold colours of JP McManus. However, the long wait was worth it, as he bounded clear of the field in a Down Royal bumper by 10 lengths from a rival who went on to land his next two outings. Sadly, that was all we got to see of Gordon Elliott's gelding but hopefully he'll make his mark in good-quality hurdling events this winter, as he's looked all class so far. GORDON ELLIOTT

ANGELS BREATH (IRE) 5 gr g

Word had clearly got out before Angels Breath made his rules debut that he might be decent, as he was sent off 6-4 favourite for the Grade 2 Supreme Trial Novices' Hurdle at Ascot. He didn't let supporters down, winning easily from some more experienced rivals, a few of whom had already won a couple of times. That performance encouraged his trainer to remark that he felt the son of Shantou was 'a bit special', and bookmakers promoted him to being one of the leading players in the market for the Supreme Novices' Hurdle. However, things didn't go to plan thereafter, as he was beaten at Kempton following a couple of months off and then didn't really feature at Cheltenham in March. He finished on a positive though, third in a 2m4f Grade 1 at Aintree, and one would imagine he'll contest some decent contests during the winter, potentially as a novice chaser. NICKY HENDERSON

ANNAMIX (FR) 6 gr g

Annamix clearly has a ton of ability – he once headed the Supreme Novices' Hurdle market without a run over hurdles – but his problem is making the track. He had one start in France for Guillaume Macaire at Vichy where he claimed second before being purchased privately to wear the famous pink and green colours of Susannah Ricci. It would be a humongous 830 days before he ran for Willie Mullins but he was still sent off an odds-on market leader. He could finish only second on that occasion but, following another 88 days away from the track, he gained a first success when beating a fair rival at Clonmel, again the well-backed market leader. Looking every inch a chaser, he clearly has a decent engine and, despite a lack of experience, one would imagine he will be seen over fences sooner rather than later. WILLIE MULLINS

APPLE'S JADE (FR) 7 b m

Although her season finished on a bit of a low note, it's hard to forget just how impressive Apple's Jade was at the start of her 2018-19 campaign. Of course, by the end of the previous year she was a multiple Grade 1 winner over a range of distances. Her return from a summer break in 2018 saw her land a Grade 2 by 11 lengths, which were followed by three starts at the top level that she won by 20, 26 and 16 lengths. She had a choice of targets at the Cheltenham Festival and connections chose the Champion Hurdle, but she was to run probably her worst race in that, beaten a long way by Espoir

D'Allen. Two more okay but below-her-best performances were next and she is left with something to prove again now, but it's hard to believe she's lost all her ability and more success is sure to come her way. GORDON ELLIOTT

ARAMON (GER) 6 b g

While it's hard to predict what Aramon will be doing this campaign, what we do know is that he wants a fast-run race on a sound surface, and is Grade 1 class when getting those conditions. He didn't appear to be anything more than a fair handicapper on the Flat in Germany for Markus Klug but was impressive on his debut for Willie Mullins, scoring with plenty in hand at Kilbeggan over 2m3f. That would be the only time he would run over that distance as the remainder of the season was spent at around 2m. His breakthrough performance came when winning a Leopardstown Grade 1 over Christmas, which he followed with a fine effort behind Klassical Dream in February. He wasn't disgraced at the Cheltenham and Aintree festivals after that but was probably over the top when well beaten at Punchestown. He could go chasing now or step up in distance again over hurdles. WILLIE MULLINS

ASK FOR GLORY (IRE) 5 b g

Paul Nicholls has plenty of promising youngsters to go to war with this season and Ask For Glory appeals as the type to develop into a smart novice hurdler. Impressive in winning both his point-to-point and bumper debut at Chepstow, he was sent off just 13-2 for the Champion Bumper but seemed to get worked up by the occasion and faded sharply having taken a strong hold through the early stages. Plenty of good horses tend to emerge from the also-rans in that event and he's just the sort to notch a sequence in novice hurdles before again winding up at the major festivals. PAUL NICHOLLS

BAND OF OUTLAWS (IRE) 4 b g

Band Of Outlaws was a fairly decent performer on the Flat for Joseph O'Brien, reaching an official mark of 93. At the end of his last campaign on the level he was gelded before being sent hurdling. He showed distinct signs of promise on his jumping debut, finishing third of 23, and he duly built on that, winning his next two. That set him up for an attempt at the Fred Winter Juvenile Handicap Hurdle, a race he won comfortably after showing a nice turn of foot. Evidently, he has plenty of class and, having finished third in the Galway Hurdle during the summer, is likely to turn up in all the valuable handicaps this season. JOSEPH O'BRIEN

BATTLEOVERDOYEN (IRE) 6 b g

Gordon Elliott enjoyed a fine season with this smart son of Doyen who racked up three wins before a disappointing effort at the Cheltenham Festival. He progressed into a top-class novice hurdler with wins at Punchestown and Naas before scoring at Grade 1 level on his return to the latter. That looked a strong renewal, with Sams Profile in second, yet he was in a different class to those rivals and it was no surprise he went off favourite against the likes of Champ and Brewin'Upastorm for the Ballymore Novices' Hurdle. He was pulled-up that day, but a line can be drawn through that effort and another big season is expected now sent novice chasing. He is clearly hugely talented, has the scope for chasing and could stay further than 2m4f. GORDON ELLIOTT

BEAKSTOWN (IRE) 6 b g

This monstrous horse is certainly made for chasing and could prove a top-class novice over fences this season. Although he was never really suited to hurdling his class was exposed by a Grade 2 Warwick win in January. That form is hard to judge as the favourite, Tidal Flow, ran very poorly but he was clear of a good second in Stoney Mountain. Beakstown would then finish pulled-up in a strong renewal of the Ballymore at Cheltenham but his real future lies over fences. He's a big, progressive type who should relish being tested over larger obstacles especially as he steps up in distance. Dan Skelton's chasing prospect has form on ground varying from good to soft and should be a top performer this year. DAN SKELTON

BIRCHDALE (IRE) 5 b g

Irish point-to-point winner in 2018 who quickly made up into a really useful novice hurdler last season. A maiden hurdle success at Warwick was followed by a Grade 2 at Cheltenham in January, albeit he had a fight on his hands with the smart Brewin'Upastorm when left clear at the last. Sent off just 6-1 for the Albert Bartlett at Cheltenham in March, he ran well for a long way, holding every chance off the final bend but got tired up the hill and his rider eased him right down late. He wasn't seen again afterwards, but very much appeals as the type to make a smart staying novice chaser and can win his share before perhaps ending up in something like the National Hunt Chase. NICKY HENDERSON

BLAZER'S MILL (IRE) 5 b g

This son of Westerner was purchased for £180,000 at the Aintree sales and remains a highly exciting novice hurdling prospect for the Olly Murphy team. The form of his lengt defeat to Birchdale in a point-to-point has worked out very strongly with that runner, trained by Nicky Henderson, already successful at Grade 2 level. A patient approach, meanwhile, was taken with Blazer's Mill, who raced only once in a bumper at Fontwell in February. He won comfortably from the front, even though he was a tad green in running, and a tough finish was enough to defeat Mount Windsor by three-and-a-half lengths. That rival has franked the form with six- and seven-length wins subsequently, meanwhile the Fontwell bumper was run over 1m5½f, and Blazer's Mill would be expected to stay much further than two miles. He looks a promising novice hurdler for the season. OLLY MURPHY

BLUE SARI (FR) 4 b g

After an impressive debut romp at Gowran Park from subsequent Punchestown winner Front View in January, Blue Sari got snapped up by legendary owner JP McManus and was chosen as the sole representative of Willie Mullins in the Champion Bumper at Cheltenham in March. The four-year-old was heavily supported and ran a cracker, finishing very much second-best to classy winner Envoi Allen. He could well go to the top over hurdles this season, with most ground expected to come alike, and the Supreme Novices' Hurdle is likely to be his long-term target. WILLIE MULLINS

BREWIN'UPASTORM (IRE) 6 b g

If one horse is owed a change in luck it is Brewin'Upastorm, who endured an unfortunate but productive novice hurdling campaign. He won with ease at Huntingdon on his hurdling debut before a fine fourth behind the talented Champ in the Grade 1 Challow Hurdle. His big victory was denied by a last-hurdle fall when in contention with Birchdale in the Ballymore Trial at Cheltenham. He would go on to run fourth in the main event itself before a fine second at Aintree behind Colin Tizzard's Reserve Tank – who would then follow up at Punchestown. Brewin'Upastorm is a chaser in the making while he remains a highly talented prospect who deserves to scoop a valuable prize. He will be sent novice chasing this year and should take a significant step forward. Perhaps he could be one for the JLT or Arkle. OLLY MURPHY

BRIGHT FORECAST (IRE) 5 b g

One would imagine that anything Bright Forecast has done to this point will turn out to be a bonus as he looks as though he's going to make a cracking chaser in time. His sole run in a point during 2018 wasn't overly exciting but he won a maiden hurdle at 20-1 on his debut for Ben Pauling and then followed that up at Leicester. Connections then sent him for a Grade 2, in which he finished second, and he improved plenty for that performance when recording a career-best upped in trip for the Ballymore, finishing third to City Island, beaten just over four lengths. It wouldn't be surprising, considering his age and experience, if he started the season over hurdles but chasing can't be far away. BEN PAULING

CAMELIA DE COTTE (FR) 7 b m

This mare enjoyed a fine campaign last year without really hitting the headlines, landing six wins from eight starts for the Mullins team. One of those defeats came to the top-class Le Richebourg at Listowel but on her last start she looked like a mare capable of troubling some of the best chasers around over 2m4f. She ran out an easy winner of a Grade 3 mares' event beating the 141-rated Pravalaguna in comfortable fashion. Seen to best effect from the front, Camelia De Cotte took a step forward with each start and this could be the season she picks up a major win, although she will need to improve again to beat the boys. WILLIE MULLINS

CAPTAIN CATTISTOCK 6 b g

Paul Nicholls' runner could develop into a fine staying handicap chaser this season having finished the year in excellent style with two wins from his last three starts. He toughed it out in a decent novice handicap at Exeter before finishing third at Uttoxeter, where he shaped as if he could be better suited to further than three miles. He made good use of an additional two furlongs when making all in eyecatching style at Fontwell, fending off the challenge of the useful Station Master in a small but quality contest. Captain Cattistock may not have been well-suited to the track that day – he is a strong galloping horse whose best form has come at Wincanton – but his class prevailed. He's a fine second-season novice chaser who will relish galloping tracks, some cut in the ground and extended distances, and a race like the Welsh National could be ideal for him. PAUL NICHOLLS

CAPUCCIMIX (FR) 6 gr g

Unraced in points and bumpers, he wasted little time in making a fine impression, winning a 16-runner maiden hurdle at Clonmel in January despite doing plenty wrong. He failed to cope with the rise in grade and step up to 3m back there next time, being eased right down, but it's worth noting he was sent off shorter than high-class, and Cheltenham Festival-winning, stablemate Minella Indo (who finished second). He very much appeals as the type to do better with a summer under his saddle. Presumably, he will begin in conditions hurdles but has the option of chasing too. Either way, he's a horse with plenty more to offer. HENRY DE BROMHEAD

CHACUN POUR SOI (FR) 7 b g

This classy ex-French chaser quickly made up for lost time, having been injured soon after joining Willie Mullins, when slamming rivals on his Irish debut in a beginners' chase over two miles at Naas in March. The seven-year-old then took the step into Grade 1 company in his stride when seeing off the top-class Defi Du Seuil in the Ryanair Novice Chase. That was a serious effort and, with another summer on his back, there should be plenty more to come yet and he is a serious Champion Chase prospect. WILLIE MULLINS

CHAMP (IRE) 7 b g

A dual Grade 1 novice winner in his second season as a hurdler last term, Champ heads into the new campaign as one of the most exciting chase prospects around. The strong-travelling seven-year-old certainly isn't devoid of pace, but he really looked the part when signing off on his first attempt at 3m during Aintree's Grand National meeting. It's as a stayer that he is really expected to shine over fences and, while rising eight, he's got relatively few miles on the clock. It just remains to be seen whether a flat track is his optimum in that sphere, otherwise the world is his oyster this term.
NICKY HENDERSON

CHANTRY HOUSE (IRE) 5 br g

In November 2014, Chantry House was purchased from the sales ring for 12,500 euros, but by the time he went through for a third time he'd landed the second of his two starts in points after unseating his rider on his debut. Current connections had to go to £295,000 to secure the son of Yeats on this occasion and noted owner JP McManus placed the gelding with Nicky Henderson. He missed a couple of engagements to kick off his career under rules due to the going but didn't disappoint when found some soft ground at Warwick, coming home a clear winner. One would imagine hurdling is now on the agenda and he's the type to pick up a few races in that discipline, almost certainly at a high level. NICKY HENDERSON

CHRIS'S DREAM (IRE) 7 b g

Although twice finishing well beaten at the major festivals, Chris's Dream has shown flashes of smart form, indeed he started out his 2018-19 season with two wins from three starts, including a Grade 2 at Navan in February. Having bypassed Cheltenham he went to Aintree for the Grade 1

over 3m, but was let down by his usually sound jumping and trailed home a well-beaten fifth of six before again flopping at Punchestown. His optimum trip remains to be seen, but he starts out his season from a mark of 146 and very much appeals as the type to come into his own this term.
HENRY DE BROMHEAD

CIEL DE NEIGE (FR) 4 b g

Willie Mullins may have classier horses in his yard, but there are sure to be plenty of opportunities for this one this season. Although winless in three attempts in France, he kept good company and there was much to like about his debut run for the yard, finishing third of 21 from a mark of 132 in the Fred Winter. He wasn't seen again afterwards, presumably as connections wanted to keep his novice status intact for this season, and he could easily rattle up a sequence before working his way into a higher grade. WILLIE MULLINS

CILAOS EMERY (FR) 7 b g

Cilaos Emery is a horse who hasn't always had things go his way. He is very lightly raced for a seven-year-old and, despite that, his form over hurdles has been extremely good, including a Grade 1 success from a stablemate in the 2017 Champion Novice Hurdle at Punchestown. He was seen only a couple more times over hurdles afterwards before making his chasing debut in early 2019. He took to fences adeptly and finished over six lengths in front of the subsequent Arkle winner but that was to be our only view of him that season. Hopefully he'll be back for this campaign, and while he won't find things easy up against more experienced types, he has the latent ability to land plenty of races if avoiding injury.
WILLIE MULLINS

CITY ISLAND (IRE) 6 b g

Despite a heavy defeat at the Punchestown festival on his final outing, City Island enjoyed a remarkable novice campaign last season. The high point came when defeating the likes of Champ and Bright Forecast in the Ballymore Novices' Hurdle at Cheltenham without previously testing himself in Graded company. It was a case of him being ready for a holiday when subsequently flopping and this hardy six-year-old no doubt has what it takes to give Paisley Park et al something to think about in the Stayers' Hurdle division. MARTIN BRASSIL

CLAN DES OBEAUX (FR) 7 b g

Clan Des Obeaux finally built on his immense potential last term, progressing into a legitimate top-class staying chaser and putting in a memorable performance when toying with his rivals en route to victory in the King George. The extended 3m2f of the Gold Cup proved too much for him on the softening ground and he was likely over the top when beaten nine lengths by the top-class Kemboy at Aintree, but there's almost certainly more to come from him again this season and the King George will presumably be his main aim, at a track that suits him ideally. Given how his trainer has excelled with numerous Gold Cup horses over the years, keeping them at the top level for multiple seasons, expect him once again to be a major force this term. PAUL NICHOLLS

CONCERTISTA (FR) 5 ch m

Concertista is a truly fascinating mare for this season. She proved to be useful in France on the Flat during 2017 for Christophe Ferland, winning a handicap over 1m2f, but was not then seen over hurdles until making her debut in the Grade 2 mares' novice hurdle at the Cheltenham Festival. Not surprisingly sent off a 66-1 chance considering the magnitude of her task, she ran a cracker, finishing second after taking to the new challenge with relish. She wasn't seen after that, presumably to preserve her maiden status, and is already a 10-1 chance for that same Cheltenham race in 2020. It seems inconceivable that she won't have won at least once by this time next year. WILLIE MULLINS

CYRNAME (FR) 7 b g

It's unlikely that you'll ever see Cyrname on a left-handed track again, as he is proving to be top-class going clockwise. The signs were always there that he was well above average – it was just a matter of putting it all together. What makes him so exciting is his racing style; he enjoys making the running and puts in some huge leaps when they are needed. The 2018-19 season didn't start off with a bang but his final two efforts of that campaign reminded everyone what he can do. He started with a 21-length demolition of his rivals from the front off a mark of 150 at Ascot, carrying 11st 10lb, before a 17-length success in a Grade 1 at the same track, utilising the same bold front-running style. Now officially rated 176 (RPR 181), he's sure to have his path laid out going in the direction he prefers, and he'll take a deal of catching wherever he turns up. PAUL NICHOLLS

DARASSO (FR) 6 br g

Although it was clear he had a smart engine, it seemed as though this ex-French performer could prove tricky to place after his first two outings for Joseph O'Brien last term. However, a decision to switch him back to fences really paid off as he mopped up a couple of Graded events over the minimum distance. That took his chasing record to three from three and this season he could prove a surprise package in the Champion Chase division for JP McManus. He acts on good to soft but excels when the mud is flying. JOSEPH O'BRIEN

DEFI DU SEUIL (FR) 6 b g

Apart from a spell between November 2017 and November 2018, when he really struggled for some reason, Defi Du Seuil has been a classy performer since joining current connections from France. His juvenile hurdling campaign was exceptional having picked up three Grade 1s including the Triumph Hurdle. Then came the lean spell, which coincided with his chasing debut. However, that first defeat over fences was soon forgotten when he won next time from Topofthegame. He was beaten in a small field afterwards, but he picked up his next two, the second of which was the JLT at Cheltenham. His final start before a summer off can be excused as he was dropped to 2m, a trip almost certainly short of his best nowadays, and he is already a leading player for the Ryanair Chase in March. PHILIP HOBBS

DELTA WORK (FR) 6 br g

The impression that the 2018 Pertemps Network Final winner left something on the table when third in the RSA Chase was confirmed in no uncertain terms as he signed off the season in style at Punchestown, cruising to a third Grade 1 success over fences. That came in a hot field, A Plus Tard was well back in third, and his jumping couldn't have been better. He has to rate as a serious Gold Cup contender heading into the new campaign, with such versatility regarding underfoot conditions a serious asset. GORDON ELLIOTT

DEPLOY THE GETAWAY (IRE) 4 b g

We've yet to see Deploy The Getaway under rules but if his 20-length demolition of 11 rivals in a four-year-old maiden point at Tallow is anything to go by, a race in which only three finished, we'll know a whole lot more about him this time next year. Sent off 3-1 favourite for that event, he was soon in front and steadily drew further and further away, recording an easy success. This all saw him become the joint-third most costly purchase at the Tattersalls Ireland Cheltenham February Sale and he looks set to run for Willie Mullins. There's no doubt he will go the usual route and start off in bumpers, and it'll be interesting to see whether new connections allow the son of Getaway stride on, something his previous trainer suggested he enjoyed doing. WILLIE MULLINS

DICKIE DIVER (IRE) 6 b g

Dickie Diver, second on his rules debut when green behind Lisnagar Oscar at Ffos Las, confirmed himself a smart sort when fourth in a gruelling edition of the Grade 1 Albert Bartlett at Cheltenham in March. However, he was very much a work in progress over hurdles, waiting to embark on a novice chase campaign, and it is this season when the six-year-old ought to really come into his own. His bloodless Irish point success came on deep going, but a sound surface is not a problem either for this dour stayer. NICKY HENDERSON

DINONS (FR) 6 b g

Dinons is a five-time hurdles winner, including at Cheltenham, and had excuses when pulled up in the Albert Bartlett in March. It didn't take him long to make an impact once switched to fences in the spring, winning on his first two attempts before running below form when last seen at Killarney in June. Ideally suited by a sound surface, expect to see him out in the autumn and he can add further wins in novice events before moving into good-quality handicaps. There are significant prizes to be won with him. GORDON ELLIOTT

DLAURO (FR) 6 b g

Finally, in May of 2019, we got to see this horse who featured as an unraced prospect in this book last year. The reason he was added 12 months ago was the fact he was purchased for a whopping £410,000 by respected connections following one start in points, where he won at Belharbour by six lengths. There was a worrying time during the winter when nothing was seen of the Lauro gelding, but Joseph O'Brien unleashed him at Punchestown, where he was sent off the 2-1 second favourite. Anyone who backed him that day didn't have the slightest moment of concern as he took it up around two furlongs out and stayed on far better than anything else, coming home 11 lengths in front of the second who, along with the third, went on to success in bumpers. The future looks very bright for Dlauro, presumably starting over hurdles this term. JOSEPH O'BRIEN

DOMMAGE POUR TOI (FR) 6 b g

Dommage Pour Toi rates a very smart novice chase prospect for the season ahead. Off the mark at the third time of asking when landing a Grade 2 at Fairyhouse in April, springing a bit of a shock in the process, he was snapped up by Gigginstown and headed for a Grade 1 at Punchestown on his final outing. Finishing fifth in what was a deep race, he shaped better than the result and the race looked to be coming soon enough in his career, but it's all about chasing with this six-year-old and he could take high rank. HENRY DE BROMHEAD

DOWNTOWN GETAWAY (IRE) 6 b g

Sold for a massive £350,000 after winning a Fairyhouse bumper for Margaret Mullins, the son of Getaway joined Nicky Henderson to go hurdling, but didn't make his debut until just over a year after the sale. Although beaten at odds-on after making a bad error three out, he still had eight subsequent winners behind him and managed to get off the mark narrowly at Ascot next time despite jumping poorly. Stepped up in both trip and class for his final start at Aintree, he dropped away tamely and ran well below previous form with others in the race. It could be that he did not stay the 3m, but that remains to be seen and he can be expected to be stronger and more streetwise this season. He has the option of switching to fences if he is deemed ready, but he needs soft ground. NICKY HENDERSON

DUC DES GENIEVRES (FR) 6 gr g

Duc Des Genievres went almost two years without a win, but showed himself to be a smart novice hurdler in defeat and the switch to fences last term was always likely to be the making of this strapping grey. A surprise reversal first time up was initially viewed as a disappointment, but it came at the hands of A Plus Tard. He stormed to festival success in March, not long after this gelding posted an equally impressive Cheltenham victory when running away with the Arkle, jumping like a pro and hammering his rivals. It may not have been the strongest edition of the race and he was a bit disappointing at Punchestown on his final outing in April, but he's very much the type to progress again this term and he ought to prove versatile trip-wise. It would be no surprise to see him end up over intermediate trips as he may be found wanting for pace in the Champion Chase division. WILLIE MULLINS

ELDORADO ALLEN (FR) 5 gr g

Colin Tizzard's charge suffered an unlucky novice campaign last season, managing only two appearances, but he made quite the impression and can certainly kick on this season. On his first start since moving from France he ran out a highly impressive maiden hurdle winner at Sandown, landing a good race in comfortable fashion. That form worked out well with the second, Sevarano, going on to be defeated only a neck by the highly talented Bright Forecast while the third that day behind Eldorado Allen, Finawn Bawn, won twice and was third at Grade 2 level. Eldorado Allen was taken to Aintree with connections viewing him as an ideal type for the Grade 1 Tolworth but he unseated his rider and did not feature that season again. His trainer insisted the injury should not cause long-term damage and he could certainly prove something of a forgotten gem. He is suited by plenty of cut in the ground and he is worth monitoring during the winter. COLIN TIZZARD

ELIXIR DE NUTZ (FR) 5 gr g

This racy five-year-old proved a complete revelation after breaking his duck at Cheltenham's November meeting last season. The switch from Philip Hobbs to Colin Tizzard appeared to have worked the oracle as that was followed by another ready win back there in December, and he landed a hat-trick in the Grade 1 Tolworth Hurdle at Sandown the following month. Sadly, connections had to draw stumps due to injury, ruling him out of a crack at the Supreme Novices' Hurdle. However, such patience is expected to pay off as he dips his toe into an open-looking Champion Hurdle division. Most ground comes alike. COLIN TIZZARD

EMITOM (IRE) 5 b g

He enjoyed a fine season last year winning four of his five starts with a sole defeat coming to the hugely talented Champ in Aintree's Sefton Novices' Hurdle. Warren Greatrex took a patient approach with him but he defeated some progressive sorts on his rise to the top level, including Lisnagar Oscar at Ffos Las and Interconnected, who was then bought for £620,000, in a hot novice contest at Newbury. He improved with every run last season and his jumping became

slicker with experience. Meanwhile, he is still a young horse so improvement is anticipated this season. Emitom is set to embark on a staying hurdling campaign and perhaps he could emulate the yard's former star Cole Harden, who landed the Stayers' Hurdle at Cheltenham in 2015.
WARREN GREATREX

ENVOI ALLEN (FR) 5 b g

Envoi Allen maintains his place in this book having been selected last year, when unraced under rules, after a big-money purchase following a ten-length win in a point. Obviously at that stage he was in here on potential but it's fair to say Gordon Elliott and his team got their money's worth in the bumper arena. He was all the rage on his debut, winning in good style as a 4-9 favourite. Connections wasted little time stepping him up in class and 14 days later he picked up a Listed event at Navan. He won a Grade 2 next, with a 48-day break in between, before finishing an unbeaten campaign with a narrow success in the Champion Bumper at Cheltenham. He ought to be somewhere near the top echelons of novice hurdlers this winter over whatever trip connections decide.
GORDON ELLIOTT

FAST BUCK (FR) 5 br g

After this two-time French Flat winner chased home smart Fakir D'Oudaries on his hurdling debut for team Mullins, when conceding best part of a stone, Fast Buck looked a certain winner. However, he flopped next time out and it wasn't until the summer that he broke through. That came in a weak affair, but he showed his true colours when following up at the Galway festival and is an interesting horse to follow this term. He could well be one for a big handicap. WILLIE MULLINS

FAUSTINOVICK 5 b g

Colin Tizzard is used to handling high-quality stock and he
looks to have another potential star on his hands in the
shape of this once-raced five-year-old. Clear second to a
smart sort on his only start in a point, it was a similar story
on his one run under rules. He made smooth and stealthy
headway from off the pace in a Newbury bumper to chase
home subsequent Grade 2 Aintree winner McFabulous, very
much looking the sort to benefit from distances in advance
of 2m once hurdling. He can start off steadily, with maiden
hurdles a possibility, but it surely won't be long before he's
competing at a higher grade and it would be no surprise
were he to end up in something like the Ballymore. COLIN
TIZZARD

FERNY HOLLOW (IRE) 4 bb g

Purchased for £300,000 by Harold Kirk for Willie Mullins,
Ferny Hollow has the sort of price tag that means success is
all but expected. He is out of the mare Mirazur, who is from
the family of Champion Hurdle- winning brothers Morley
Street and Granville Again. In common with many expensive
horses in this book, he did his impressing in Irish points, this
one landing a 2m4f four-year-old maiden at Knockanard in
February 2019 by 15 lengths, keeping on powerfully in the
latter stages for then-trainer Colin Bowe. Expect this son
of Westerner to be all the rage when making his debut in
bumpers and there is little doubt he has the ability to rack up
a few wins in that discipline. WILLIE MULLINS

FUSIL RAFFLES (FR) 4 b g

Fusil Raffles arrived late on the Triumph Hurdle scene last
term, only making his British debut at Kempton in February,
but such was the impression he created when storming to
success in the Adonis that he jumped straight towards the

head of the market for the Cheltenham event. Unfortunately, he failed to make it due to an injury picked up at the final flight of his Kempton win. He did manage to recover in time for Punchestown and offered a case of what might have been as he breezed to a first Grade 1 success. Highly regarded and very much expected to be a better horse with a clear run this upcoming season, he's certainly an interesting Champion Hurdle candidate in a division lacking depth. NICKY HENDERSON

GALVIN (IRE) 5 b g

Gordon Elliott does particularly well at keeping all of his owners happy, no matter what level their horses operate at, and Ronnie Bartlett must have been pleased with how Galvin was placed last season. Unraced before his rules debut, he started off in a bumper in July 2018 and won that event. He followed that up with another win in that company before picking up a maiden and two novice hurdles, two of which came in Scotland. It was easy to begin thinking that the gelding was merely useful without being anything special and connections were just targeting weak events to build up a winning profile. However, he soon dispelled that theory when he looked unlucky not to finish closer in the Grade 1 Ballymore Hurdle at Cheltenham in the spring. Conditions were too sharp for him on his final run before a summer off and it's not difficult to envisage the son of Gold Well landing plenty more races this season. GORDON ELLIOTT

GARDENS OF BABYLON (IRE) 4 b g

Joseph O'Brien enjoyed a productive juvenile hurdling campaign with this son of Camelot, winning two races before a promising third behind Pentland Hills in the Triumph Hurdle. That placed effort was quite eyecatching as he made up a fair bit of late ground, suggesting he may be better over an extra half-mile this year. He then raced in Grade 2 company when beaten half a length by the useful French Made, but he jumped poorly that day so to even go that close shows he is a horse with plenty of natural ability. Gardens Of Babylon was disappointing when last seen in the Galway Hurdle but there should be much more to come from him this season, and if he can improve his jumping there's no reason why he can't become a smart hurdling prospect. JOSEPH O'BRIEN

GET IN THE QUEUE 5 b g

This unbeaten son of Mount Nelson will always be remembered for being the last winner ridden by top jockey and the now-retired Noel Fehily but he could have a bright future too now stepping out of bumpers. He made a huge impression when winning by nine lengths on his debut at Uttoxeter and followed it up with a similarly comfortable win at Exeter. While his Newbury win, at odds of 1-3, was somewhat of a novelty, it is worth remembering the Harry Fry yard target that prize with their better bumper horses and he drew clear of the talented Prince Llywelyn in good style. Though not the strongest renewal of that particular bumper, Get In The Queue remains a hugely exciting prospect especially now he tackles hurdling. HARRY FRY

GLORY AND FORTUNE (IRE) 4 b g

It shows the regard in which Glory And Fortune is held that Tom Lacey tested him in a Cheltenham Listed race on his debut and he duly delivered with a superb four-and-a-half length win. It had been reported that Glory And Fortune was impressing his trainer before the run on New Year's Day and his class prevailed as he drew clear from two horses (Cascova and Book Of Invasions) who had won previously. He is a big horse and Lacey has taken a patient approach with him, missing the spring festivals of Cheltenham and Aintree. He may start his hurdling career at a low grade before slowly rising up through the ranks but he remains an outstanding novice hurdling prospect who could make his presence felt at Graded level. TOM LACEY

GOOD BOY BOBBY (IRE) 6 b g

Nigel Twiston-Davies has taken a patient approach with this exciting chasing prospect but he did little wrong in four starts over hurdles. He won fairly ordinary races at Carlisle, Southwell and Ffos Las but shaped with improvement on each start and this could be the year he competes at Graded level. He was last seen defeating the 127-rated Quoi De Neuf by seven lengths at Ffos Las when carrying 12st 1lb, which was a very solid effort. His sole defeat came to the talented Remastered but a line can be drawn through that effort as he never quite travelled with his usual imposing class. He seems to handle all grounds, is a naturally talented horse and remains a top-class prospect as a novice chaser this season. NIGEL TWISTON-DAVIES

GYPSY ISLAND (IRE) 5 b m

Gypsy Island made it four wins from as many starts in bumpers when romping home in a Grade 3 at the Punchestown festival on her final outing last season. The classy mare has a serious engine and is settling better these days. Racing too freely was the mitigation offered for her sole defeat, when making her hurdling debut at Navan, but trainer Peter Fahey has always maintained she'd make up into a top jumper. Her pedigree suggests stepping up in trip won't be a cause for concern, and she is definitely one for top honours as the campaign develops. PETER FAHEY

HAZZAAR (IRE) 5 b g

Hazzaar never quite reached the heights expected of him last season having made just two starts but he certainly looks a novice hurdler to keep onside this season. He made a big impression on his debut in an Ascot bumper when running out a comfortable winner, and the form has worked out well with Prince Llywelyn, two lengths behind in second, going on to finish the same spot at Listed level. Hazzaar, meanwhile, would then be sent off favourite in Ascot's typically competitive December Listed bumper. He disappointed when seventh, although he pulled hard and was reported to have been too free by Aidan Coleman. He did not run again that season but should be better suited to going over hurdles this term. TOM LACEY

HONEYSUCKLE 5 b m

Not many had the mare Honeysuckle on their list of horses to follow around a year ago, plenty wouldn't have even known her name, but the daughter of Sulamani may well be one of the stars of the 2019-20 season judged on what we've seen so far. She was a 15-length winner of a four-year-old mares' maiden point-to-point in April 2018 and changed hands four days later for 110,000 euros. New connections didn't bother with bumpers and she won a 2m4f mares' maiden hurdle on her opening start for them by 12 lengths. Then followed a mares only 2m Listed novice event before a six-length Grade 3 success in similar company upped to 2m2f. She concluded that campaign with a five-and-a-half-length victory in the top company for her sex, impressing again with the manner of how she destroyed her rivals over 2m4f. One would imagine that it will be Grade 1s all the way now and she is easily one of the most interesting mares to follow this winter. HENRY DE BROMHEAD

IF THE CAP FITS (IRE) 7 b g

Harry Fry's gelding bounced back from an injury that curtailed his novice hurdle season with pretensions of being a Champion Hurdle contender. However, he ran into the smart Verdana

Blue in a couple of races over a sharp 2m and looked more of a stayer when having to dig deep to take the Ascot Hurdle in between. He then struggled around Fontwell's sharp turns in the National Spirit Hurdle, which resulted in him bypassing Cheltenham. It was no surprise to see him stepped up in trip on his final start, when contesting the Grade 1 Ryanair Stayers' Hurdle at Aintree, and he was also fitted with cheekpieces for the first time. He travelled much better this time as a result and proved very game, overcoming a last-flight blunder to just get the better of Roksana and Apple's Jade in one of the races of the season. That performance marks him out as a potential Stayers' Hurdle candidate, unless connections decide to go chasing this season. The only question is how he will handle the undulations when tackling Cheltenham for the first time. HARRY FRY

INDEFATIGABLE (IRE) 6 b m

The mares' division is more competitive these days, but Paul Webber's likeable six-year-old has already established herself as one of the best around, finishing fifth in the mares' novice at Cheltenham, and her final outing back at the same venue in April saw her improve for the step up to 2m4f, winning with ease despite a poor round of jumping. There will be a plethora of opportunities for her over hurdles this term and she should prove to be a real money-spinner. PAUL WEBBER

JON SNOW (FR) 4 br g

Having got off the mark at the third time of asking over 1m4f on the level in France, Jon Snow was subsequently gelded and snapped up for a hurdling campaign in the pink and green silks of Susannah Ricci, under the expert tutelage of Willie Mullins. Out of a half-sister to Champion Hurdle winner Binocular, he should stay no bother and winter ground isn't expected to pose any problems. WILLIE MULLINS

KALASHNIKOV (IRE) 6 br g

The winner of a Betfair Hurdle and runner-up in a Supreme
Novices' Hurdle during his novice hurdle season, Kalashnikov
was immediately switched to fences last term. He made a
good start, winning at long odds on in ordinary contests at
Warwick and Plumpton, but was subsequently beaten in Grade
2s at Kempton and Ascot, which rather dented his reputation.
He was deprived of a chance to restore it in the Arkle at
Cheltenham, as he was badly hampered when Ornua fell and
he lost his rider. Stepped up in trip for the Grade 1 Manifesto
Novices' Chase at Aintree, he showed his true colours when
beating a field of talented rivals. He seems much happier
going left-handed, as he has yet to score in three tries on
right-handed tracks, and the Ryanair Chase is a sensible aim.
AMY MURPHY

KEMBOY (FR) 7 b g

A French-bred son of Voix Du Nord, Kemboy really progressed
over fences last season. He now must be considered one of
the best chasers in the British Isles and a major contender for
the top honours this campaign. He won four of his five starts,
including the Grade 1 Savills Chase at Leopardstown, the
Betway Bowl at Aintree and the Punchestown Gold Cup. He
beat the Gold Cup winner in the latter contest, suggesting he
might have gone close at Cheltenham but for an unlucky
first-fence departure. Still only a seven-year-old, he looks likely
to be aimed at the same major races he contested last season
and will be hard to beat. WILLIE MULLINS

KING ROLAND (IRE) 5 br g

Patience might end up being the keyword associated with King
Roland. Winner of his sole start in points for Sophie Lacey, he
moved to Harry Fry for racing under rules some 265 days later.
He was fitted with a hood for his bumper debut and bolted

up by 22 lengths at Uttoxeter, making his rivals look like second-raters in the process. Given a couple of months off to get over that effort, he was sent off a 4-9 shot at Ffos Las and carried his penalty to success by a length. That success saw him receive quotes of around 16-1 for the Champion Bumper but he did not take up that engagement. Hopefully, he will be on the track early to run in some novice hurdles, and if he takes the promise he's shown already to jumping he could easily develop into a festival horse for next spring. HARRY FRY

KLASSICAL DREAM (FR) 5 b g

Klassical Dream failed to win over hurdles in France but kept strong company and everything fell right when he joined Willie Mullins last season. He began by winning a 20-runner maiden hurdle at Leopardstown over Christmas and then rattled off a Grade 1 hat-trick, including a commanding victory in the Supreme Novices' Hurdle and a similarly impressive display at Punchestown when last seen. He heads into this season as a legitimate Champion Hurdle contender. Klassical Dream could develop into another Faugheen, though without the jumping frailties, and we'll learn more about his credentials as his metal is tested in some of the recognised trials. He is expected to take high rank in a division ripe for domination.
WILLIE MULLINS

L'AIR DU VENT (FR) 5 b g

Colin Tizzard has enjoyed much success for Brocade Racing, primarily with Gold Cup hero Native River, and they could have another potentially smart sort on their hands courtesy of this five-year-old. He won his only start in a bumper at Bangor last season, scoring with considerable ease having been strong in the market before the off. He had earlier fallen in a point-to-point having travelled well with fellow 100 Winners member and impressive bumper winner Shiskin, and it will be fascinating to see how far he can progress in novice hurdles up to 3m this season. COLIN TIZZARD

LAURINA (FR) 6 b m

Beaten on both her starts in France for Guillaume Macaire, Laurina quickly established herself as a top-class racemare for Willie Mullins. She was imperious on her Irish debut, ploughing through the mud at Tramore to win a maiden hurdle by 15 lengths. From then on during that novice campaign it was Graded company, and she collected a top-level success when over eight lengths too good for her rivals at Fairyhouse. Last season opened with a very easy success in a match race against a vastly inferior rival before she comfortably took the Quevega Mares' Hurdle on her next run. Connections then decided it was finally time for her to take on the geldings, and she ran okay in the Champion Hurdle, finishing a well-held but respectable fourth. Fences should be an option now, but it would be no surprise were she kept to hurdling in the short term to see if she can do even better up against the boys. WILLIE MULLINS.

LISP (IRE) 5 ch g

Lisp failed to greet the judge again after a successful comeback last season, but he still ran some blinders in Graded handicaps thereafter and the suspicion is the best of him is yet to be seen. The five-year-old has time on his side, might well appreciate a stiffer test now and is well up to landing a big pot when the mud is flying this term. Connections also have the option of switching to fences. ALAN KING

LOSTINTRANSLATION (IRE) 7 b g

This imposing performer had been waiting to jump a fence last term and it was little surprise that he managed to break through at the top level as a novice chaser. That came against a below-par Topofthegame during Aintree's Grand National meeting when signing off, but an RPR of 165 was fully warranted. His slick jumping ought to hold him in good stead when taking on the big boys this season on a trail towards the Gold Cup, and the King George VI Chase at Kempton on Boxing Day looks tailormade. COLIN TIZZARD

MALONE ROAD (IRE) 5 b g

This good-looking five-year-old made £325,000 at the Aintree sales after easily winning on his Irish point debut in 2018, going to Cheveley Park Stud and trainer Gordon Elliott. He justified odds of 2-5 without breaking sweat on his rules debut at Down Royal later in the year, but was even more impressive when smashing rivals at Punchestown next time. That saw him awarded an RPR of 135, but sadly injury struck and he was forced to miss a crack at the Champion Bumper. Elliott remains confident he can put that behind him when tackling novice hurdles this season, though, and it'll take a serious performance to lower his colours. GORDON ELLIOTT

MCFABULOUS (IRE) 5 b g

Bought for 88,000 euros in June 2017, McFabulous is certainly bred to be decent considering he's a half-brother to two winners, most notably Waiting Patiently. Unlike plenty of youngsters, he didn't have any tries in points and was pitched into bumpers as a four-year-old. Punters clearly weren't expecting too much on his debut as he was allowed to go off 13-2, but that didn't stop him registering an impressive winning debut at Chepstow. The next run, in a Listed event, wasn't good but that was to be his only blip, as he won both starts after, ending with a Grade 2 victory at Aintree. That race produced hurdling winners before this book was published so Paul Nicholls must be chomping at the bit to send the son of Milan over timber this season. PAUL NICHOLLS

MELON 7 ch g

Now must be the time to send Melon chasing. He burst on to the scene as an exciting novice but didn't progress as seemed likely, although he did produce plenty of big performances in defeat, most notably finishing second twice in the Champion Hurdle plus filling the same position in the Supreme Novices' Hurdle prior to that. Connections have experimented with headgear and distance which, in the main, hasn't worked so fences are surely beckoning now. Should he take to them, there must be every chance he'll be a leading candidate for the Arkle come March. WILLIE MULLINS

MIDNIGHT SHADOW 6 b g

Best forgiven a flop in the Grade 2 Cleeve Hurdle on Trials Day at Cheltenham in January, Midnight Shadow heads into the new campaign as a seriously exciting novice chase prospect. The Relkeel Hurdle winner has been biding his time before tackling fences and ought to excel at around 2m4f for Sue and Harvey Smith. He doesn't want it too testing underfoot and the JLT looks an ideal long-term target. SUE SMITH

MIN (FR) 8 b g

There have been various times across the years when a horse is unlucky to be around while a true champion is racing, and Min is arguably one of those with Altior proving the immovable object. Willie Mullins has been able to steer his horse away from that challenger on plenty of occasions, and he shows his class more often or not. For instance, there were three Grade 1 successes last season and he gained a new career-best when slamming Politologue by 20 lengths at Aintree. At the age of eight, he's not going to be getting any better but it's possible the 2m chasing division will be for the taking if, as expected, Altior heads up in distance. Quotes of around 12-1 for the Queen Mother Champion Chase may look extremely generous come March. WILLIE MULLINS

MINELLA MELODY (IRE) 5 b m

A ten-length winner of her sole point-to-point, this daughter of Flemensfirth established herself as a very useful bumper performer last spring. She ran out a clear-cut winner of a point-to-point bumper at Gowran Park and was then asked to contest the Grade 2 mares' bumper at Aintree. She was sent off favourite but lost out there to The Glancing Queen. She was also beaten at Punchestown but has still done quite well in her short time racing, and this close relative of the smart Glens Melody looks a decent prospect for novice hurdles this time around. HENRY DE BROMHEAD

MINELLA INDO (IRE) 6 b g

There are few better trainers than Henry de Bromhead when it comes to chasers and Minella Indo rates a top-class novice prospect for the season ahead. A relative unknown at the beginning of last season and defeated on his first two starts over hurdles, he caused what appeared a huge shock when winning the Albert Bartlett at 50-1 in March, but his performance was one of sheer dominance, travelling oh so strongly and galloping on relentlessly up the hill to reverse form with old rival Allaho. He put to bed any fears that was a fluke when following up in the Grade 1 staying novice at Punchestown, again putting Allaho in his place, and the prospect of him jumping a fence this season is highly exciting.

He's expected to take some stopping in Ireland before crossing the water to compete in the RSA. HENRY DE BROMHEAD

MYSTICAL CLOUDS (IRE) 6 gr g

Alan King's six-year-old has been a bit of a slowburner, winning just one of his eight starts so far in bumpers and hurdle races, but chasing was always likely to be the making of him and hopefully he will get his chance to jump the larger obstacles this term. Assuming that is the case then look for him to win a novice handicap chase or two, with a step up to 3m likely to be within range. ALAN KING

NEVER ADAPT (FR) 4 ch f

Never Adapt had a memorable start for the wrong reasons in Britain last season when third in the Triumph Hurdle trial at Cheltenham in November. She raced extremely keenly, dragging Barry Geraghty to the head of affairs, flying clear in the early stages before being caught out by the talented Quel Destin and Cracker Factory in a muddling race. She did fight back to grab third from Katpoli but it was her inexperience that lost her the race. There is no doubting she is very talented and it was not hard to envisage her beating subsequent top-level winner Quel Destin if she settled, and she was even made favourite for the Triumph after that run. She suffered an injury that led to her missing the rest of the season but she is a talented prospect who could be worth following.
NICKY HENDERSON

ONE FOR ROSIE 6 gr g

After winning on his bumper debut, this grey gelding was not seen for over a year. However, once he began his hurdling career, he progressed nicely and looks a decent stayer in the making. A win over 2m4f at Carlisle on good ground was followed up by a lesser effort on soft at the same track, when the mud found him out. He bounced back on a sounder surface to score at Warwick, then proved he could handle a softer surface by losing out in a close finish to the Grade 3 EBF Novice Hurdle Final at Sandown, when carrying top weight. Stepped up to Grade 1 company on his final start at Aintree, he put in another solid performance to dead-heat for third place. He gives the impression that 3m will not trouble him and he could improve further at that trip. It would not be the biggest surprise, though, if he went novice chasing this term. NIGEL TWISTON-DAVIES

ORNUA (IRE) 8 ch g

There are few better sights in horse racing than watching a trailblazing chaser let rip over 2m and Ornua put on a show on plenty of occasions last season as a novice. A winner four times, his finest moment came when landing the Grade 1 Maghull at Aintree's Grand National meeting. He ran too free and made costly fencing errors on his final outing at Punchestown, but he will no doubt be placed to good effect in small-field graded races this season, including in Britain where he is a familiar visitor. HENRY DE BROMHEAD

PAPA TANGO CHARLY (FR) 4 ch g

The French-bred four-year-old caused quite a stir when comfortably landing an Irish point at Liscarroll in March and was subsequently snapped up for a whopping £440,000 to join resurgent trainer Jonjo O'Neill for a campaign under rules. Now owned by the yard's new sponsor, he's got a lovely pedigree and will be expected to win his bumper first time up, before connections then decide whether to crack on over hurdles. Soft ground is no problem and he'll appreciate a good test. JONJO O'NEILL

PIC D'ORHY (FR) 4 b g

A smart juvenile hurdler in France, finishing placed at
Grade 1 level, Pic D'Orhy joined Paul Nicholls last season
with quite the reputation and made his British debut in the
Triumph Hurdle. He ran better than his finishing position of
tenth implies – travelling strongly, he was essentially let down
by his jumping. Chasing is likely to be his game this season,
and he can enjoy a weight-for-age allowance to begin with,
and it would be no surprise were he to make it at a very high
level. PAUL NICHOLLS

PRECIOUS CARGO (IRE) 6 b g

A fairly useful bumper performer for Lucinda Russell, the
son of Yeats was switched to Nicky Henderson to begin his
hurdling career. He was seen only three times, winning nicely
at Kempton on his hurdling debut before following up in
effortless style at Sandown. His trainer then set him a big task
by stepping him up in class to contest a Grade 1 novice hurdle
at the Grand National meeting. He found things happening
a bit too quickly for him there, but he was not given a hard
time when his chance had gone, and that kindness may
pay off in time. An imposing horse and an accurate jumper,
he looks sure to make a better chaser than a hurdler. He
can be expected to win his share in that sphere. NICKY
HENDERSON

REAL STEEL (FR) 6 b g

Willie Mullins' novice improved steadily throughout last
season, ultimately looking like a top-class prospect over
fences. He took chases at Fairyhouse and Thurles before
decent efforts when tested at Grade 1 level in the JLT and
in the Ryanair Novices' Chase at Fairyhouse – finishing
sixth and second respectively. But it was at the Punchestown

festival where he stamped his class, defeating his novice handicap rivals in impressive fashion off a mark of 151. His trainer won that race with Kemboy, who would prove to be a Grade 1 three-mile chaser, the previous year, and perhaps this runner will benefit from being tested over a longer trip. Real Steel is a progressive type who can step up this season, while he is ground-versatile and has plenty of class. WILLIE MULLINS

RESERVE TANK (IRE) 5 b g

It's very fair to suggest that after Reserve Tank's first two starts, no one could have predicted he'd finish his first season as a two-time Grade 1-winning hurdler. He wasn't asked to run in bumpers and instead made his debut in a Chepstow novice hurdle, being beaten almost six lengths into a modest third. His next outing ended up being worse but then his run of success began. Winning at Sandown by just over two lengths, he managed to register a fairly impressive RPR of 136. Those first three runs had been over about 2m, but he was stepped up five furlongs next time, and narrowly beat a Nicky Henderson-trained gelding handing him weight. Three weeks later he was sent to Aintree for his first effort at the highest level and won that by just over three lengths, before another win in the Champion Novice Hurdle at Punchestown. It seems more than likely he will go chasing now, where further success seems assured. COLIN TIZZARD

ROAD TO RESPECT (IRE) 8 ch g

Road To Respect is the sort of horse everyone would love to own. Consistent throughout his whole career, often at the highest level nowadays, he wins at least once a season no matter what sort of opposition he's pitched against. Last year's success came on his first start of the campaign in the

JNWine.com Champion Chase, an unsurprising achievement to his fans as he's often found his best form when fresh. Indeed, the three times he's run following at least 180 days off he's won. Although he didn't add any more victories to his haul last year after Down Royal, he continued to run with credit and gained a new career best RPR of 171 when finishing third in Cheltenham's Ryanair Chase. Look out for him again this season, especially on his seasonal return. NOEL MEADE

SALDIER (FR) 5 b g

Saldier began last season as a potential Champion Hurdle prospect having rounded off his juvenile campaign with a Grade 1 win at the Punchestown festival. But, having taken a heavy fall on his reappearance, plans were shelved and he wasn't seen again. That reappearance came at Naas in a four-year-old hurdle in which his main market rival was a certain subsequent Champion Hurdle winner, Espoir D'Allen. Saldier looked to have him in a spot of bother, going best coming to the last, only to depart. Throw in the fact Willie Mullins' charge was conceding weight, with the pair well clear, and connections must have been left wondering what if. Hopefully he is over whatever injury kept him off track for the remainder of the season. He very much heads into this season as a forgotten horse. WILLIE MULLINS

SAMCRO (IRE) 7 ch g

Adding Samcro to this book could go either way. He may bounce back to his brilliant best or continue to struggle at whatever level he's pitched into. The first seven times he set foot on the track under rules he won, landing two Grade 1s, the second of which was the Ballymore Novices' Hurdle at the Cheltenham Festival. That's unfortunately when the run of success ended. He fell on his final start of that campaign and started the last one with a surprise defeat at Down Royal. Buveur D'Air then readily disposed of him in the Fighting Fifth Hurdle before a tame effort at Leopardstown over Christmas. That was the last time he ran in the 2018-19 season, although a return to the track was mooted at various points during the spring. Gordon Elliott will need to work his magic as attention is switched to chasing, but Samcro remains a horse of superstar potential. GORDON ELLIOTT

SAMS PROFILE 5 b g

Mouse Morris has a real star chasing prospect on his hands in Sams Profile. He put in a huge performance to go down by half a length to Aintree Grade 1 winner Reserve Tank at Punchestown. The son of Black Sam Bellamy was tested at a good level throughout the year including when a fair second to Battleoverdoyen at Naas and a solid fifth in the Ballymore Novices' Hurdle at Cheltenham in advance of his brave effort in Punchestown's Champion Novice Hurdle. Sams Profile should improve massively for being sent over fences and he could prove a smart prospect in the novice division this year. He handles most ground. MOUSE MORRIS

SANTA ROSSA (IRE) 5 b m

This mare was a surprise winner on her bumper debut, but proved it was no fluke by developing into a high-level performer in that division last season. She was a much shorter price when staying on strongly to win a Grade 2 mares' bumper at Leopardstown next time, encouraging connections to go to Aintree and take on the geldings. She ran well to finish third behind McFabulous, despite being a little keen on the softer ground, and was subsequently sent to Punchestown for the Grade 1 bumper. Again taking on geldings, she performed creditably but was short of room and got bumped in the closing stages. She will go novice hurdling this season, and can be expected to make her mark, particularly when taking on her own sex. DERMOT A MCLOUGHLIN

SANTINI 7 b g

This Grade 1 Sefton Novices' Hurdle winner was restricted to just three outings as a novice chaser last term, but still made it to the RSA at the Cheltenham Festival and ran a blinder when pushing Topofthegame to less than a length up the famous run-in. Nicky Henderson left him off for a summer break afterwards and hopes are high that, with a smoother campaign, this grand-looking seven-year-old will have few peers as he heads towards a tilt at the Gold Cup this season. Soft ground suits ideally. NICKY HENDERSON

SHISHKIN (IRE) 5 b g

Sporting the colours worn by notable horses with Willie Mullins, namely Melon and Al Boum Photo, Shishkin debuted for Nicky Henderson in March 2019 and looked every inch a star in the making. Before that, he'd had two outings in points, winning the second of them by eight lengths before going through the sales ring for £170,000. Word had obviously got out before his opening start under rules that he was well above average as bookmakers sent him off a 4-6 shot for his bumper, and he performed how all odds-on shots should, in no danger from some way out and winning easily. A gelding with size about him, he can only get stronger with age and should develop into a smart hurdler. NICKY HENDERSON

SPIRITOFTHEGAMES (IRE) 7 b g

The consistent Spiritofthegames can land a valuable handicap chase this season for the Dan Skelton team. He was a useful handicapper over the smaller obstacles, finishing third in the Betfair Hurdle and fifth in the County Hurdle and adjusted well to the chasing last year. He won a Listed prize at Chepstow in October and went on to finish third in two valuable handicaps at Cheltenham, including behind the progressive Siruh Du Lac at the festival. Although he was well beaten in a Grade 1 at Aintree, he remains open to improvement as a second-season chaser and is more than capable of exploiting his current mark of 150. DAN SKELTON

THE GLANCING QUEEN (IRE) 5 b m

Fifth in the Champion Bumper at the Cheltenham Festival, The Glancing Queen confirmed her status as one of the best mares around when readily winning back against her own sex in Grade 2 company at Aintree the following month. That came on bad ground, but she did win a Listed event on good going and is clearly versatile in that regard. Alan King will be plotting a route back to Cheltenham over hurdles this season, and she ought to prove hard to beat along the way.
ALAN KING

THOMAS DARBY (IRE) 6 b g

A half-brother to the smart hurdler Muirhead among others, this lightly raced six-year-old proved a useful recruit to hurdles last season. He impressed when beating the subsequent Grade 1 Tolworth Hurdle winner Elixir Du Nutz on his hurdling debut, but lost out at Ascot next time when racing too keenly and then making a bad mistake at the third-last. He was again too keen when beaten in the novice hurdle at Kempton on Boxing Day, before receiving a confidence booster at Taunton. He was an outsider for the Supreme Novices' Hurdle at Cheltenham but was suited by the good gallop, which enabled him to settle. He handled the soft ground well and ran on to be second behind the awesome Klassical Dream. He was reportedly lame afterwards but has hopefully recovered and looks the type to improve. He seems to prefer good

ground, but handles soft, and might even be sent chasing this season if connections deem him ready.
OLLY MURPHY

TOP VILLE BEN (IRE) 7 b g

A second season chaser who could scoop a nice staying handicap this season is the Philip Kirby-trained Top Ville Ben. Proving himself a fine three-miler last season, he destroyed fields at Hexham and Wetherby (twice) and finished a respectable third in an Aintree Grade 1 behind the potential Gold Cup candidates Lostintranslation and Topofthegame. He has a mark of 151, which could make him competitive in the prestigious big-field events, while he handles cut in the ground and looks the sort who could relish races requiring seemingly limitless stamina. He looks to favour left-handed tracks and, although he fell in the RSA Chase, Cheltenham could be ideal for the son of Beneficial.
PHILIP KIRBY

TOPOFTHEGAME (IRE) 7 ch g

If you're going to break your duck as a novice chaser, there's no better place to do it than the RSA at the Cheltenham Festival – and that's exactly what played out for Paul Nicholls' Topofthegame. In arguably the race of the meeting, this giant chestnut gelding saw off Santini and Delta Work under a fine ride by Harry Cobden. It all clicked into place that day and he proved himself in the stamina department, despite the race not being as severe a test as can often be the case. He was ready for a summer holiday when failing to fire at Aintree's Grand National meeting on his final outing, and Nicholls is unsurprisingly confident that the seven-year-old has what it takes to bring the Gold Cup back to Ditcheat for the first time since Kauto Star won the race in 2009. PAUL NICHOLLS

TOWER BRIDGE (IRE) 6 b g

Having only made four unsuccessful starts over fences, the Joseph O'Brien-trained son of High Chaparral has retained his novice status for the season. A former Grade 1 scorer over hurdles, he was learning on the job when well beaten on two occasions before then running a fine second to subsequent Arkle winner Duc Des Genievres at Gowran Park. He once again bumped into a top-class prospect at Cheltenham when A Plus Tard destroyed his field in the Close Brothers Novices' Handicap Chase but Tower Bridge was a fine second that day with the third, Ben Dundee, well behind. There is still plenty more to come from him over fences and he may improve on better ground too – he could land a valuable pot this year or perhaps even step up into Graded novice level.
JOSEPH O'BRIEN

WEST APPROACH 9 b g

As a half-brother to the great Thistlecrack it is no surprise that West Approach has proved a real talent over hurdles and fences. He had some strong pieces of chasing form last year including a third at Cheltenham and fifth in the Ladbrokes Trophy, while over hurdles he finished second to the brilliant Paisley Park in the Long Walk and Cleeve Hurdles. He may not win at Graded level but he is rated 140 over fences, compared with his rating of 150 over hurdles, and considering he has run well in big-field handicaps it is only a matter of time before he has his turn. He was subject to a mammoth gamble from 25-1 to 5-1 for the bet365 Gold Cup, but finished only sixth. Perhaps he could reward his backers through 2019 and into 2020. COLIN TIZZARD

WALK AWAY (IRE) 6 b g

Henry de Bromhead has no end of promising novice chase
prospects for the season ahead and this six-year-old is high up
the depth chart. A point winner in December 2018, he made
an impressive debut under rules when easily coming clear to
win at Thurles by nine lengths in March. He then coped well
with a steep rise in grade when finishing fourth to Champ in
the Grade 1 Sefton Novices' Hurdle at Aintree's Grand National
meeting just a month later. He struggled behind high-class
stablemate Minella Indo at Punchestown on his final outing,
but chasing was always going to be the making of him and,
after just three runs under rules, there's still no telling how
good he might be. It is quite possible that he could end up in
a race such as the RSA, having won his share in Ireland along
the way. HENRY DE BROMHEAD

WIDE RECEIVER (IRE) 4 b g

Gordon Elliott was clearly taken with the Tattersalls
Cheltenham Sale top lot and this son of Sholokov is now in his
care. Having cost current connections £410,000, it is surprising
to look back and notice that Wide Receiver didn't even start
market leader for his only point-to-point. Allowed to go off
5-1, he clearly knew his job and easily landed a 2m4f four-
year-old maiden, quickening up in good style. This was more
than enough to entice potential owners, all of whom were
willing to pay a whopping price tag to secure him. Naturally,
a fierce bidding battle ensued. His new handler orchestrated
an unbeaten campaign, including the Champion Bumper, for
another horse from the same sale a year earlier, Envoi Allen.
Although Wide Receiver was marginally more expensive, he
will do exceptionally well to live up to his predecessor. That
said, he is in the right place to give it a good go. GORDON
ELLIOTT

INDEX

100 WINNERS
HORSES TO FOLLOW 2020

Companion volume to *100 Winners: Jumpers to Follow*, this book discusses the past performances and future prospects of 100 horses, selected by Raceform's expert race-readers, that are likely to perform well on the Flat in 2020.

To order post the coupon to the address below or order online from **www.racingpost.com/shop**

ORDER FORM

Please send me a copy of **100 WINNERS: HORSES TO FOLLOW 2020** as soon as it is published. I enclose a cheque made payable to Raceform Ltd for **£5.99** (inc. free p&p).

Name (block capitals) ....

Address ....

....

Postcode ....

SEND TO: 100 WINNERS FLAT 2020 OFFER, RACEFORM, SANDERS ROAD, WELLINGBOROUGH, NORTHANTS NN8 4BX [100F20]